DANIEL'S DEN

5 Bedtime Stories of Lionhearted Faith

BLUME POTTER

INTRODUCTION

In the quiet moments before bedtime, the stories we share with our children and grandchildren have the power to shape their hearts and minds, leaving lasting impressions of faith, courage, and love. Daniel's Den: 5 Bedtime Stories of Lionhearted Faith is a collection crafted with this sacred time in mind.

These stories take the timeless biblical tale of Daniel in the lions' den and bring it to life through the eyes of the very lions who witnessed a miracle. As the lions encounter Daniel and experience the divine protection he receives, your little ones will learn about the power of faith, the wonder of God's protection, and the importance of trust in Him.

Each story is designed to not only captivate the imagination of your children or grandchildren but also to instill in them valuable lessons that will strengthen their faith. With its gentle, yet powerful narrative, Daniel's Den is more than just a bedtime storybook—it's a spiritual treasure that will inspire both you and the young ones you love.

As you share these stories, you'll find that they are not just about a man and some lions, but about the transformative power of God's love, making this book a must-have for every Christian home. Embrace these moments of connection and let these stories of lionhearted faith become a cherished part of your family's bedtime routine.

CHAPTER ONE:
THE MYSTERIOUS STRANGER

In the heart of the great city of Babylon, beneath the starry night sky, a den lay hidden—a den where mighty lions prowled. These lions were fierce and strong, their roars echoing through the walls. They were the king's protectors, feared by all who knew of them.

One night, as the lions settled into their usual routine, something unusual happened. The heavy stone above their den was rolled away, and a dim light from the outside world spilled in. The lions, startled by the noise, looked up and saw something they had never seen before—a man was being lowered into their den.

This man was not like the others who had been thrown into the den before. Those people had always screamed and cried, trembling with fear. But this man was different. He was calm, steady, and quiet. His eyes, though tired, were filled with a peace that puzzled the lions.

The lions, curious and confused, watched him closely. Their instincts told them to roar, to show their power, but something held them back. The man did not flinch or tremble. He simply stood there, looking around the den with a calmness that the lions had never seen in a human before.

The biggest of the lions, a mighty beast with a golden mane, took a step closer, sniffing the air. There was something unusual about this man, something that made the lion pause. The others, sensing the same, circled the man cautiously, their sharp eyes observing every move.

But the man didn't move. Instead, he knelt down, closed his eyes, and began to whisper words that the lions could not understand. His voice was soft, gentle, like the sound of a breeze rustling through the trees. The lions, who were usually ready to pounce at the slightest sound, found themselves strangely calm. It was as if an invisible shield surrounded the man, protecting him from harm.

The lions exchanged confused glances. They had never encountered a human who wasn't afraid of them. They didn't understand why, but deep down, they felt that this man was different. He was not just any human—he was special.

As the night wore on, the lions settled down around the man, still watching him with curious eyes. They didn't roar or growl; instead, they lay quietly, feeling a strange sense of peace. The man remained in prayer, unshaken by their presence.

And so, the lions kept their distance, their confusion growing with each passing moment. They couldn't explain it, but they knew that this man, this mysterious stranger, was protected by something far greater than they could understand.

The night passed, and the lions, still puzzled, drifted into a peaceful sleep, with the man resting safely in their midst. The den was quiet, filled only with the sound of calm breathing—both human and lion alike.

Little did they know, this was just the beginning of a night that would change everything.

CHAPTER TWO:
THE NIGHT OF MIRACLES

The night deepened, and the den grew colder. The lions, usually restless and ready to pounce, found themselves in a strange state of calm. They had never encountered a man like this before—a man who showed no fear, even in the presence of such mighty beasts.

As they lay around Daniel, the lions continued to watch him, their golden eyes wide with curiosity. The man hadn't moved from his place since he was lowered into the den. Instead, he remained still, his lips moving softly in prayer. There was a sense of peace around him that the lions couldn't understand, but they felt it deeply, like a warm blanket wrapping around them.

The biggest lion, who had approached Daniel earlier, tried once more to follow his instincts. He rose to his feet and took a step toward the man. But as he did, a powerful feeling washed over him—an invisible force that made him stop in his tracks. It wasn't fear; it was something different, something that made the lion hesitate, as if he knew that harming this man was impossible.

The other lions felt it too. One by one, they attempted to approach Daniel, but each time, they were met with the same invisible force. It was as if a protective barrier surrounded the man, keeping him safe from their claws and teeth. The lions exchanged bewildered glances, their confusion growing with each passing moment.

As the night wore on, the lions became aware of a presence in the den—something far greater than themselves. It was a presence that filled the space with a warmth and light that the lions couldn't see but could feel deep within their hearts. It was this presence that kept them at peace, that stopped them from acting on their instincts.

For the first time, the lions felt something they had never known before—humility. They realized that they were in the presence of a power much stronger than their own. This man, who prayed so calmly, was not alone. He was protected by a force that the lions could not comprehend, a force that filled the den with a sense of awe and wonder.

As the hours passed, the lions no longer saw Daniel as prey. Instead, they began to see him as something else—someone special, someone to be respected. They moved closer, not with the intention to harm, but with a desire to protect. The mighty beasts that had once been feared by all were now transformed into silent guardians, watching over the man with a reverence they didn't fully understand.

The night that began with confusion and curiosity had turned into a night of miracles. The lions, who had once been predators, were now protectors, and the den, once a place of fear, had become a place of peace.

Daniel, still deep in prayer, remained untouched. The lions, sensing the divine presence that surrounded him, lay down quietly around him, keeping him safe through the night.

And so, the night of miracles continued, with the lions and Daniel resting together in perfect harmony, under the watchful eyes of a power that neither beast nor man could fully grasp.

CHAPTER THREE:
THE GUARDIAN ANGEL

As the night stretched on, the lions in the den continued to marvel at the peaceful man in their midst. They had never seen anything like this before—an unshakable calmness in a place where fear usually ruled. But something even more extraordinary was about to happen, something that would forever change the way the lions understood the world around them.

As the lions lay quietly around Daniel, a soft, radiant light began to fill the den. The lions lifted their heads, their eyes widening as the light grew brighter. They weren't afraid of this light; instead, it brought a sense of calm that soothed their hearts even more.

Out of this glowing light, a figure began to take shape. It was unlike anything the lions had ever seen—a being of pure light and warmth. The figure was tall and majestic, with wings that shimmered like the morning sun. This was no ordinary visitor; the lions instinctively knew they were in the presence of something holy, something beyond their understanding.

The figure was an angel, sent to protect Daniel. The lions could feel the angel's power, but it was a power that didn't frighten them. Instead, it filled them with a deep sense of awe and reverence. The angel's presence was calming, as if the very air in the den had become lighter and filled with peace.

The biggest lion, who had tried to approach Daniel before, now felt an overwhelming urge to bow his head in respect. The other lions did the same, their once fierce eyes now soft and filled with wonder. They knew that this being was here to protect the man who prayed so calmly, and they understood that they were a part of something much greater than themselves.

The angel moved closer to Daniel, standing between him and the lions, but there was no need for any barriers. The lions had already been transformed by the presence of the angel. They no longer saw Daniel as prey but as someone under divine protection, someone they were meant to keep safe.

As the angel watched over Daniel, the lions settled down once more, surrounding the man in a protective circle. The den, which had once been a place of danger, was now filled with a peaceful silence. The lions, in the presence of the angel, felt a deep sense of purpose. They were not just predators; they were now guardians, chosen to witness this miraculous event.

The night passed slowly, with the angel's light never fading. The lions, who had started the night confused and curious, were now filled with a quiet reverence. They understood that Daniel was no ordinary man—he was someone special, protected by forces they could not see or fully understand.

As the first light of dawn began to creep into the den, the angel's form began to fade. The lions watched as the light slowly disappeared, leaving them once again in the dimness of the den. But the peace that the angel had brought remained. The lions knew they had witnessed something miraculous, something that would stay with them forever.

The night had been one of awe and transformation, with the lions coming to understand the power of faith and the incredible ways that God protects those who trust in Him. As they lay down beside Daniel, they knew that they were not alone in that den—they had been in the presence of a guardian angel.

CHAPTER FOUR:
THE MORNING LIGHT

The first rays of dawn began to filter into the den, gently brushing against the stone walls and warming the air. The lions, who had spent the night in a state of calm, stirred as the light grew brighter. They blinked and stretched, their powerful bodies slowly coming to life after the miraculous events of the night.

Daniel, who had remained in prayer throughout the night, also began to stir. The lions watched him closely, their eyes reflecting a mixture of curiosity and respect. They could sense that the night had changed everything—this was no ordinary man, and they had been a part of something far greater than themselves.

As the morning light filled the den, the heavy stone above began to move. The lions looked up as it was slowly rolled away, allowing the light to pour in fully. They knew what was coming—Daniel was going to be lifted out of the den. But unlike other mornings, there was no sense of hunger or frustration. Instead, the lions felt a strange sense of relief and wonder.

The ropes were lowered, and Daniel was gently pulled up, his face calm and his eyes still filled with that unshakable peace. The lions watched in silence, their powerful paws resting on the cool stone floor. They could feel the significance of the moment, knowing that they had witnessed something extraordinary.

As Daniel was lifted out of the den, the lions felt a quiet understanding settle over them. They had been part of a miracle, a moment where the usual rules of their world had been changed by something greater than they could comprehend. The fear and confusion they had felt at the beginning of the night were gone, replaced by a deep sense of awe.

The biggest lion, who had been the first to sense something different about Daniel, let out a soft, almost reverent sound. It was not a roar, but a gentle acknowledgment of what they had all experienced. The other lions responded with quiet murmurs, their powerful voices softened by the understanding that mercy had been shown that night—both to Daniel and to them.

As the den grew quiet once more, the lions remained still, basking in the morning light that now filled the space. They knew they would never forget this night, the night when a man of unshakable faith had come into their den and left unharmed. They had seen the power of God's protection, and it had changed them forever.

The morning light continued to shine, bright and warm, as the lions lay down to rest. The den, once a place of fear, had become a place of peace and wonder. The lions, now guardians of a miracle, understood the mercy that had been shown, and they would carry that knowledge with them always.

CHAPTER FIVE:
THE KING'S DECREE

As the morning light continued to bathe the den, the lions lay quietly, their minds still processing the extraordinary events of the night. Above them, the sounds of the city waking up filtered down, but the den remained a place of calm and reflection.

The lions' attention was soon drawn to the entrance of the den, where a new sound echoed—voices, but not the usual harsh orders of guards. These voices were filled with a sense of reverence and awe. The lions listened closely, curious about what was happening.

From the voices, the lions learned that King Darius had made a decree. The king, who had witnessed Daniel's miraculous survival, was now proclaiming to the entire kingdom that the God of Daniel was the true and living God. The lions, who had seen the power of this God firsthand, understood the significance of this moment.

The den, once a place of fear and punishment, had now become a place of worship. The lions felt a deep sense of pride and humility, knowing that they had been part of something much bigger than themselves. They had played a role in God's plan, and the den where they had once ruled with fear was now a place where God's power was honored and praised.

The biggest lion, the leader of the pride, lifted his head and let out a low, reverent growl. The others followed, their voices joining together in a harmonious sound that filled the den. It was their way of acknowledging the decree, of honoring the God who had protected Daniel and transformed their den into a sacred place.

As the day went on, the lions continued to reflect on the events of the night and the king's decree. They understood that the miracle they had witnessed had far-reaching consequences, not just for Daniel, but for the entire kingdom. The message of faith and trust in God would spread, and the lions were humbled to have been part of that message.

The den, once a place of darkness and fear, was now filled with light—both from the morning sun and from the presence of God's protection. The lions, who had once been feared predators, had become witnesses to a miracle, and they would carry the memory of this night with them always.

As the day drew to a close, the lions settled down, their hearts at peace. They knew that their den would never be the same again. It had become a place of worship, a testament to the power of faith and the impact of trusting in God. And as they rested, the lions felt a deep sense of contentment, knowing that they had been part of something truly extraordinary.

The king's decree echoed in their minds, a reminder that even the fiercest of creatures could be instruments in God's plan. The lions, now guardians of a holy place, understood the true meaning of faith, redemption, and the power of God's love.